The Best of

Shirley Thompson

QUILTING PATTERNS

Compiled by **Cheryl Barnes**

Located in Paducah, Kentucky, the American Quilter's Society (AQS) is dedicated to promoting the accomplishments of today's quilters. Through its publications and events, AQS strives to honor today's quiltmakers and their work and to inspire future creativity and innovation in quiltmaking.

EDITOR: HELEN SQUIRE
TECHNICAL EDITOR: CHERYL BARNES
GRAPHIC DESIGN: LYNDA SMITH
COVER DESIGN: MICHAEL BUCKINGHAM

PUBLISHED BY AMERICAN QUILTER'S SOCIETY
IN COOPERATION WITH GOLDEN THREADS.

Library of Congress Cataloging-in-Publication Data
  Thompson, Shirley.
    The best of Shirley Thompson quilting patterns /
    Compiled by Cheryl Barnes.
       p. cm.
    ISBN 1-57432-864-6
     1. Quilting--Patterns 2. Machine quilting--Patterns.
    I. Barnes, Cheryl. II. Title.

    TT835.W4834 2004
    746.46'041--dc22

                                2004016621

Additional copies of this book may be ordered from the American Quilter's Society, PO Box 3290, Paducah, KY 42002-3290; Toll Free: 800-626-5420, or online at www.americanquilter.com.

Dedication

To Shirley Thompson, a pioneer with the foresight to recognize a growing need in the quilting industry for unique quilting patterns. This book celebrates the 25th anniversary of Shirley's first book, *The Finishing Touch*, and her influence on the quilting industry. Her pattern books encouraged future designers and helped open the door to a whole new era, in which quilting the quilt has become a recognized outlet of creative expression.

Table of Contents

Introduction

Shirley Thompson began designing over 25 years ago. Since then, there has been a swing from the opinion that hand quilting was the only truly acceptable way to finish a quilt to the overwhelming acceptance of machine-quilted quilts. If you want evidence of this, just visit a major quilt show and count how many quilts are machine quilted and notice the range of categories recognizing the accomplishments of today's machine quilters.

I have chosen to honor Shirley with the release of this pattern book – *The Best of Shirley Thompson* – and by reintroducing her quilting patterns in an updated computer-generated version. These 200 patterns have been selected from all seven of her books to create a unique collection that highlights her distinctive style of designing for both hand and machine quilters. Her hundreds of patterns were originally hand drawn using small dashed lines. This compilation of designs has been digitized to be symmetrical and to fit into your blocks and borders with precision. They have been accurately resized to fit the most commonly sized blocks and borders. I take no credit for the designing of the patterns.

Shirley's first books were created for use by hand quilters. She had a vast knowledge of quilting and saw a new trend developing, and was among the first to begin designing continuous-line patterns for the machine quilter. Hand quilters soon discovered how easy continuous-line designs were to stitch. The stitching path of a continuous-line pattern moves from its starting point until it completes the whole design without causing the quilter to stop in one area and restart in another.

The dashed pattern shown here is a traditional feather that requires stopping and starting while stitching. The solid feather pattern shown at the top is a continuous-line design. Every feather has its own in and out stitching line so the whole design can be completed without stopping.

As you flip through the patterns, notice that some have stitching diagrams which illustrate the stitching paths as well as the starting points. Some of the designs are single and some are double lines. When this happens, the lines will look different (one will be solid and one will be dashed). Stitch the inside solid line first. Refer to page 9 for illustrated examples.

Shirley shared quilting fundamentals as well as instructions for marking, basting, and quilting in each of her books. I have expanded her ideas with updated tips and techniques that will be helpful for beginning and experienced quilters alike.

I became fascinated with quilting designs as a longarm quilter. My favorite part of the process was "playing" with patterns while considering how they would enhance the look of the customer's quilt. I hope you learn to enjoy the process of selecting and auditioning quilting patterns. Do not rush through this creative time – explore all the options until you feel you have chosen the perfect quilting designs.

My wish is that you will use the patterns in this book as your creative springboard to take your quilting to the next level and that you will enjoy exploring the endless possibilities.

Happy Quilting,

Planning & Auditioning Quilting Patterns

Planning and auditioning patterns is easier if you can view the whole quilt top. Hang the quilt top or spread it out on a flat surface while looking through the patterns in this book and considering the areas to be quilted. It helps to do this over the course of several days or while you are working on another project. Remember, do not rush this process.

- Consider the following when *planning patterns:*

    1. Is the quilting to be done by hand or machine?

    2. Who is the quilt for and does it have a theme?

    3. How will the quilt be used?

    4. Are the fabric and piecing traditional or contemporary?

    5. Is the quilting to be an important part of the overall design?

- Audition patterns using *Golden Threads Quilting Paper*, a lightweight transparent vellum*. Trace the patterns on the GT paper, then position them on the quilt top. It is best to choose several design options to audition before making the final decision.

- Watch for secondary patterns that can appear when quilting patterns are placed next to each other. Four blocks can become one large pattern or the area between two blocks can create a sashing effect.

- When selecting and auditioning patterns for odd-shaped areas, it helps to first trace the outline of the area on GT paper and then place the selected patterns within the outline, checking for the proper fit.

- Consider the following while *auditioning patterns:*

    1. Do the block and border patterns complement each other?

    2. Are the patterns too ornate or too simple for the quilt top?

    3. Is there enough quilting for the type of batting used?

    4. Will the fabric allow the quilting to been seen?

    5. Is the pattern sized to fit in the area properly?

- *Pathways to Better Quilting* by Sally Terry is an excellent resource that guides quilters as they develop the confidence to make design choices.* Sally offers methodical checklists and techniques for choosing designs, auditioning patterns, and balancing the quilting. Her methods benefit both new and experienced quilters and I recommend her book.

*See Resources, page 110.

Multiple repeats of the same design can create secondary patterns.

Resizing Quilting Patterns

- Quilting patterns may be resized on a copy machine or scanner. Check the copyright statement on the book or packet for the designer's permission to use and change the size of the patterns.

- To accurately resize patterns, the percentage of increase or decrease will need to be figured. Two sets of measurements are needed.

1. Measure the quilting pattern at its *widest* point. Borders should be measured from the *highest* point on the top of the border to the *lowest* point on the bottom. Keep in mind that these may be in two different sections of the pattern. Drawing guidelines above and below the border will make this easier to measure.

2. Measure the blocks and borders on the quilt top from seam to seam. Quilting patterns should fit into the block areas allowing at least ¼" to ½" margin on all sides. Border patterns should have the same margins plus an extra ¼" to ½" on the outside of the border to compensate for the binding. The seam to seam measurement minus the margin is your second measurement.

- Use these measurements to determine the percentage of increase or decrease. A calculator can be used. Example: The original block design measures 5″ square, and it needs to be 7″ square for the project. The calculations will be 7÷5 = 1.4 then multiply x 100 =140. The percentage of increase is 140%.

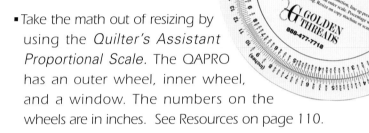

- Take the math out of resizing by using the *Quilter's Assistant Proportional Scale*. The QAPRO has an outer wheel, inner wheel, and a window. The numbers on the wheels are in inches. See Resources on page 110.

- Using the same example, locate the 5″ mark on the inner wheel and turn the wheel until it lines up to the 7″ mark on the outer wheel. Look in the window – the arrow will be pointing to 140, which is the percentage of increase.

- Audition the resized pattern to make sure the new pattern fits the area to be quilted correctly. Simply trace the resized pattern onto *Golden Threads Quilting Paper* and place it over the block or border and check the margins. This copy can then be used as the original for creating tearaway stencils using the No-Marking Method.

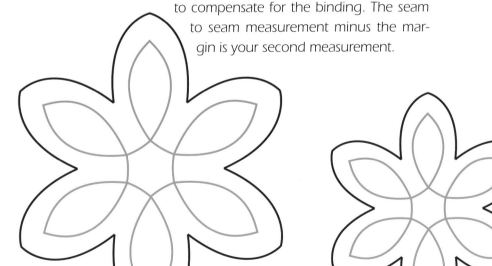

135%

100%

65%

Quilting patterns can easily be resized to fit the area to be quilted.

No-Marking Method

- The No-Marking Method uses *Golden Threads Quilting Paper*, a lightweight, transparent vellum to create tearaway stitchable stencils. This method reduces the time spent marking the fabric before stitching and removing the marks after stitching, while eliminating the worry of leaving permanent marks on the quilt top.

- Trace a pattern onto a piece of GT Paper using a wash-away marking pen, chalk pencil, or permanent fine point marker. It is helpful to mark arrows along the stitching path when the pattern has sections that cross over or change direction.

- Layer up to 15 pieces of paper with the traced copy on top and pin or staple the corners to secure. Needle punch through the stack with a large unthreaded needle. You may choose to save the traced copy to create another set of patterns.

- Consult your sewing machine instructions for stitching without thread, or trick your machine into stitching without thread. If the machine has a bobbin sensor, insert an empty bobbin in place; if the sensor is the threading path, place a business card in that area.

- Notice that one side of each needle-punched stencil is smooth and the other side has bumps. Place the bumpy side up as you pin the stencil on your quilt.

- A good light source is usually all that is needed to see the stitching path. If stitching on a light colored fabric, lightly brush the bumps with a pounce pad containing colored chalk. The raised bumps will hold just enough color for you to see the design clearly.

- Pin or use a temporary spray adhesive (see Resources, page 110) to position the tearaway stencils onto the quilt top. Spray the paper, *not the fabric*, while being careful not to spray on the stitching line or area.

- To remove the paper after quilting, grab hold of the project close to the quilted area and tug on the bias. The paper will crack away from the stitches making it easy to pull off, or remove it with a hose vacuum cleaner.

- Intricate patterns often isolate small sections of paper and may take a bit more time to remove. Use a sticky lint roller or a toothbrush to loosen and remove any small slivers of paper.

- The *No-Marking Method* also works for hand quilting and embroidery. Trace designs on the GT paper with a nonpermanent marker/pencil. Pin or spray in place and stitch through the paper, following the pattern. Remove by carefully tearing away the paper.

TRACE the design on GT paper.

STITCH with unthreaded needle.

QUILT following the holes.

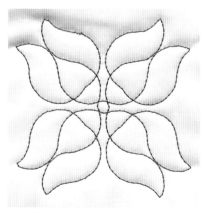
TEAR paper from quilted area.

Marking Tips

- Always mark the quilt patterns on the quilt top before you sandwich and baste the layers together. Use a chalk pencil, pre-tested washaway pen, or other removable marking tool. If a lead pencil is preferred, use a number 3 or 4 semi-hard pencil, as these give a thin marking line and will not smudge like a soft pencil. Care should be taken to mark lightly and always test markings on a sample piece of the same fabric used in the quilt.

- Stencils can be created from the patterns in the book. Trace the pattern on plastic template material and cut using a stencil cutter or burner. Check your local quilt shop for other options.

- Tulle or bridal netting can be used to transfer a pattern. Choose tulle/netting with small holes and minimum stretch. With a fine point permanent marker trace the pattern on the netting creating the stencil. Pin in place and trace the design onto the fabric through the holes of the netting with a removable marker.

- Light boxes are indispensable when marking. Place the pattern on the bed of a light box. Position the fabric on top, then trace the pattern. A light table can be created by placing a lamp under a glass table or a dining room table that has the leaves pulled apart and a piece of glass over the opening.

- Dark or busy fabric can also be marked with a light box by tracing the pattern onto a piece of black construction paper or light-weight cardboard. Punch holes following the pattern with a large darning needle. Place this dark paper on top of the light box and place the quilt top over it. The light shines through the holes, making it possible to trace the pattern through the fabric by following the "light dots." This unique tip was shared by Shirley in one of her first books.

Patterns for Hand & Machine Quilting

Continuous-line quilting patterns enable the marking and stitching of a pattern to flow freely for both hand and machine quilters. Hand quilting **designs can easily be adapted** to continuous line for machine quilting. Remember less stopping and starting means your quilting is completed quickly and easily. It will become easier to choose patterns for hand or machine quilting as your confidence grows. With over 200 patterns to select from, your own personal style will begin to develop as you use the quilting patterns in this book. At quilt shows, look closely at the different effects that hand, traditional, and longarm quilting have on the finished piece. Take notes on patterns, threads, and techniques that catch your eye, then envision incorporating them into your own quilting.

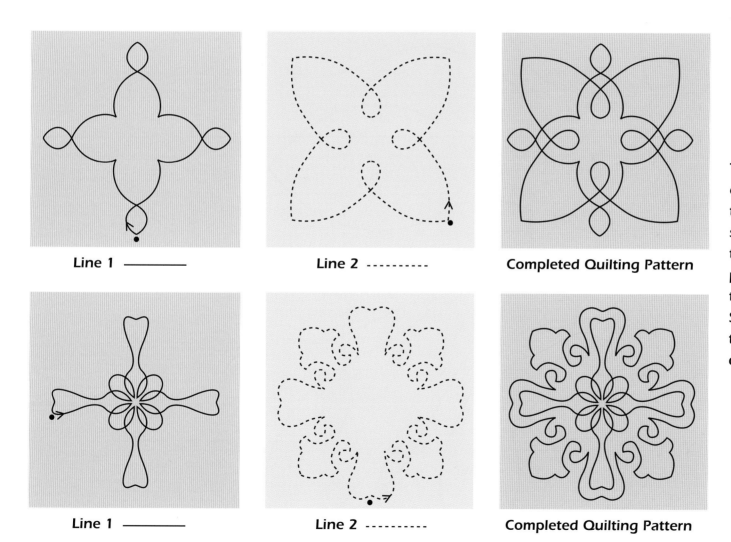

Line 1 ———

Line 2 ----------

Completed Quilting Pattern

Line 1 ———

Line 2 ----------

Completed Quilting Pattern

Two dozen small diagrams throughout this book illustrate starting points and the stitching paths for patterns with one to two lines of stitching. Stitch the solid line first then the dotted line to complete the pattern.

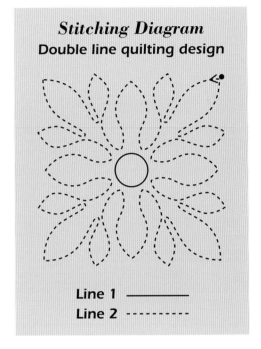

Stitching Diagram
Double line quilting design

Line 1 ———————
Line 2 - - - - - - -

by **Cheryl Barnes** – *The Best of* **Shirley Thompson** Quilting Patterns

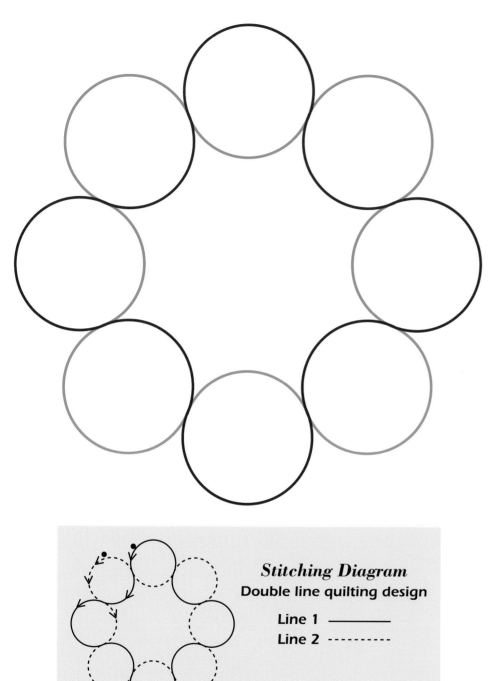

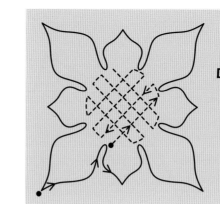

Stitching Diagram
Double line quilting design

Line 1 ———————
Line 2 - - - - - - - - -

by **Cheryl Barnes** – *The Best of* **Shirley Thompson** Quilting Patterns

Stitching Diagram
Single line quilting design

Quilting designs make great appliqué motifs.

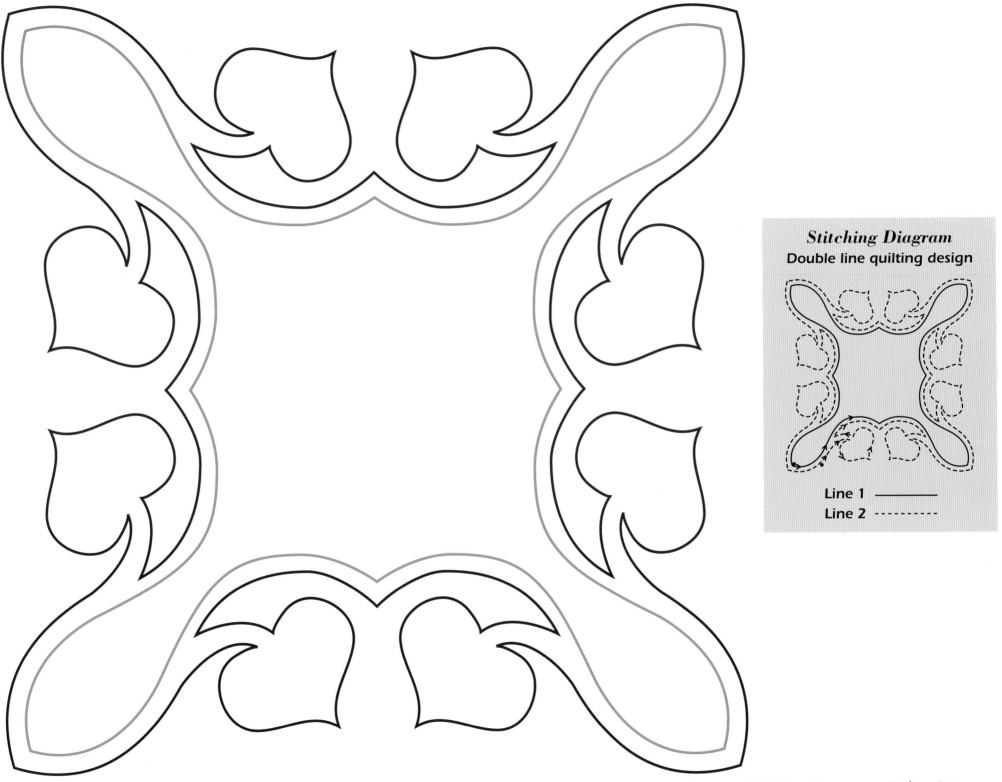

Stitching Diagram
Double line quilting design

Line 1 ———
Line 2 -------

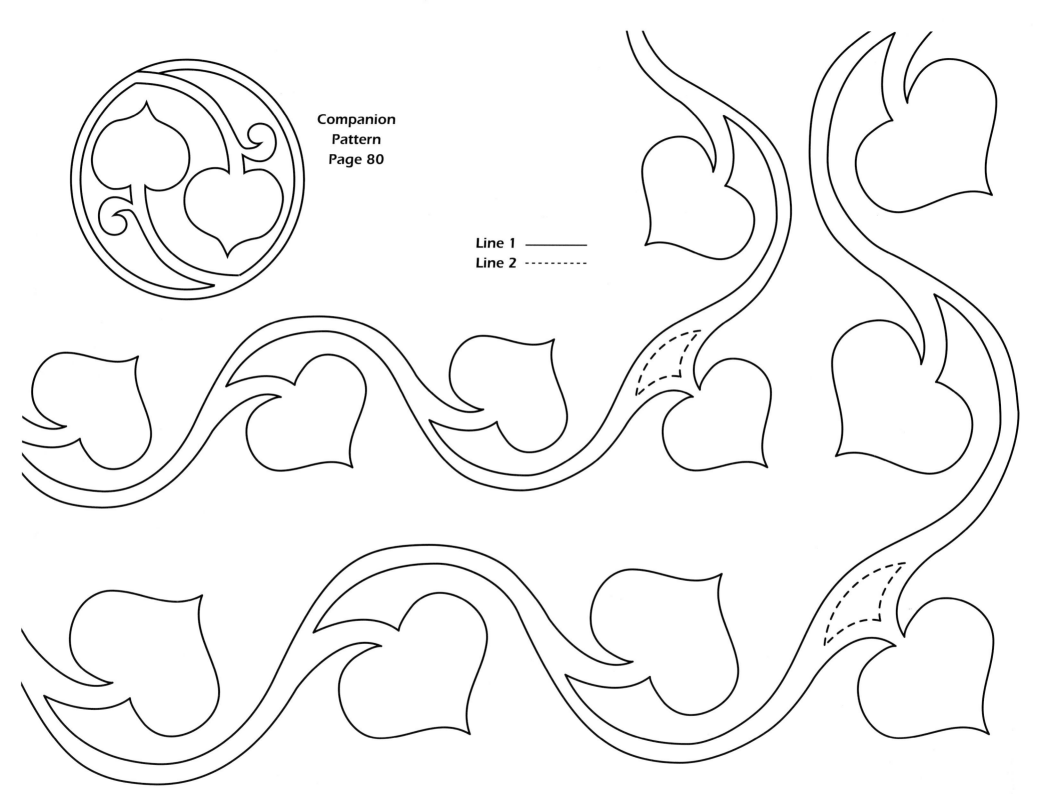

Companion
Pattern
Page 80

Line 1 ———
Line 2 ---------

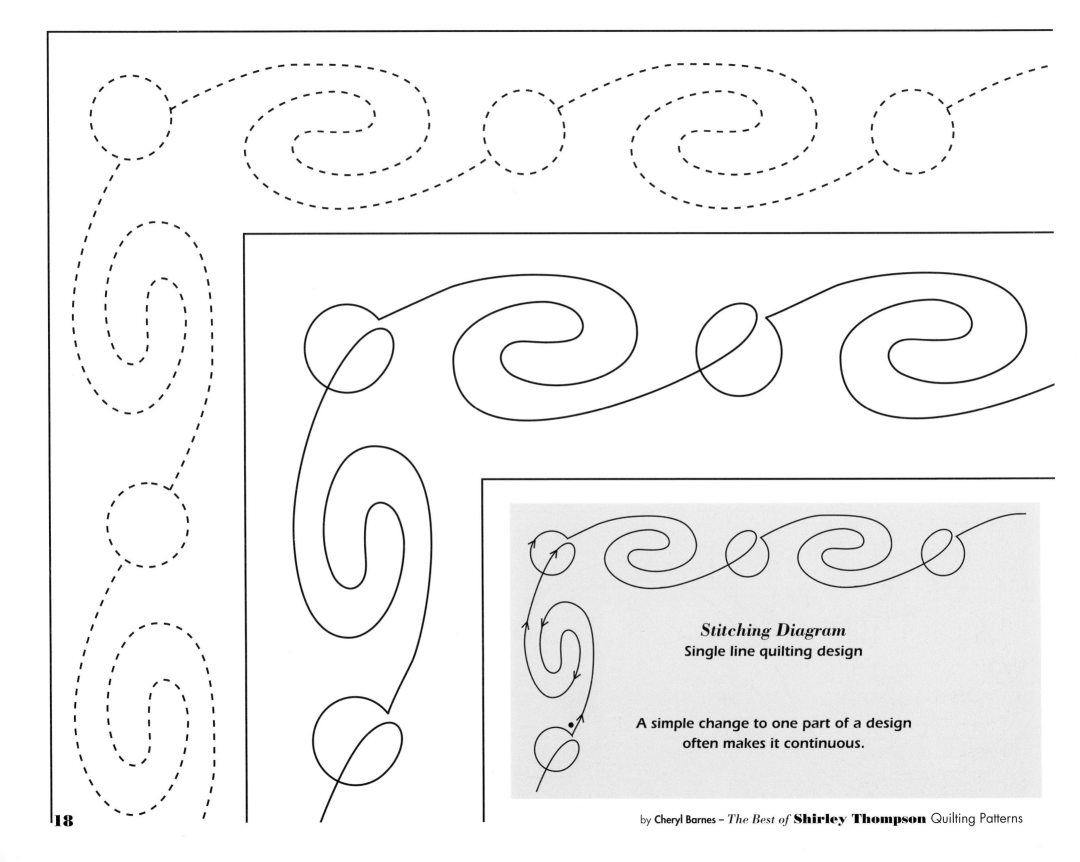

Stitching Diagram
Single line quilting design

A simple change to one part of a design
often makes it continuous.

Stitching Diagram
Double line quilting design

Line 1 ——————
Line 2 ------------

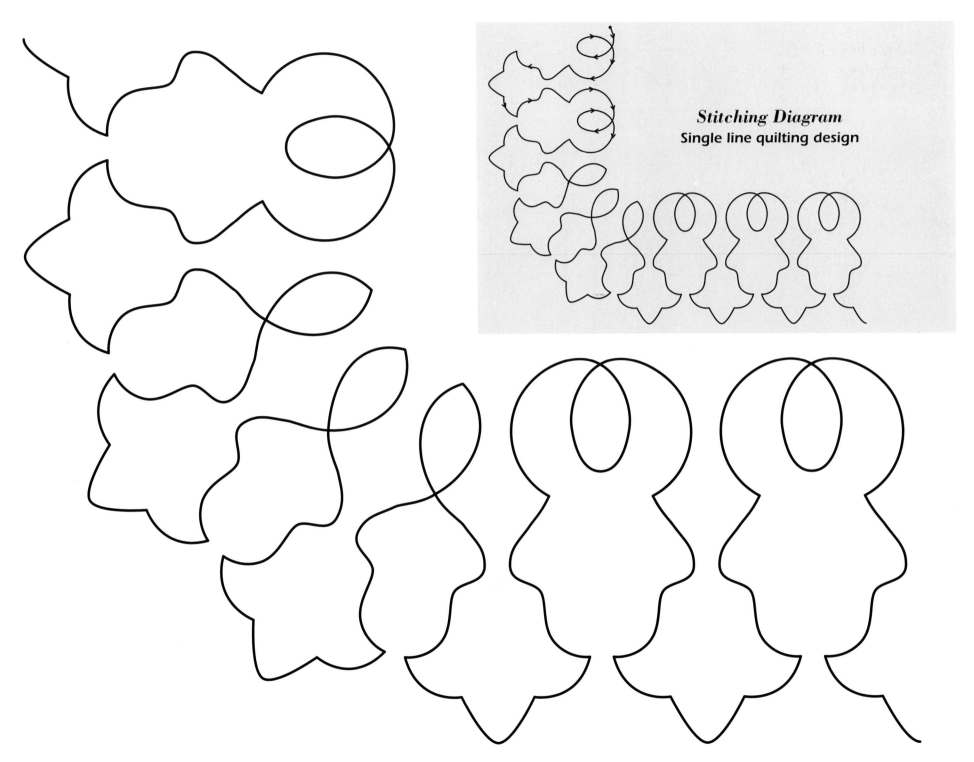

Stitching Diagram
Single line quilting design

Stitching Diagram
Single line quilting design

Stitching Diagram
Single line quilting design

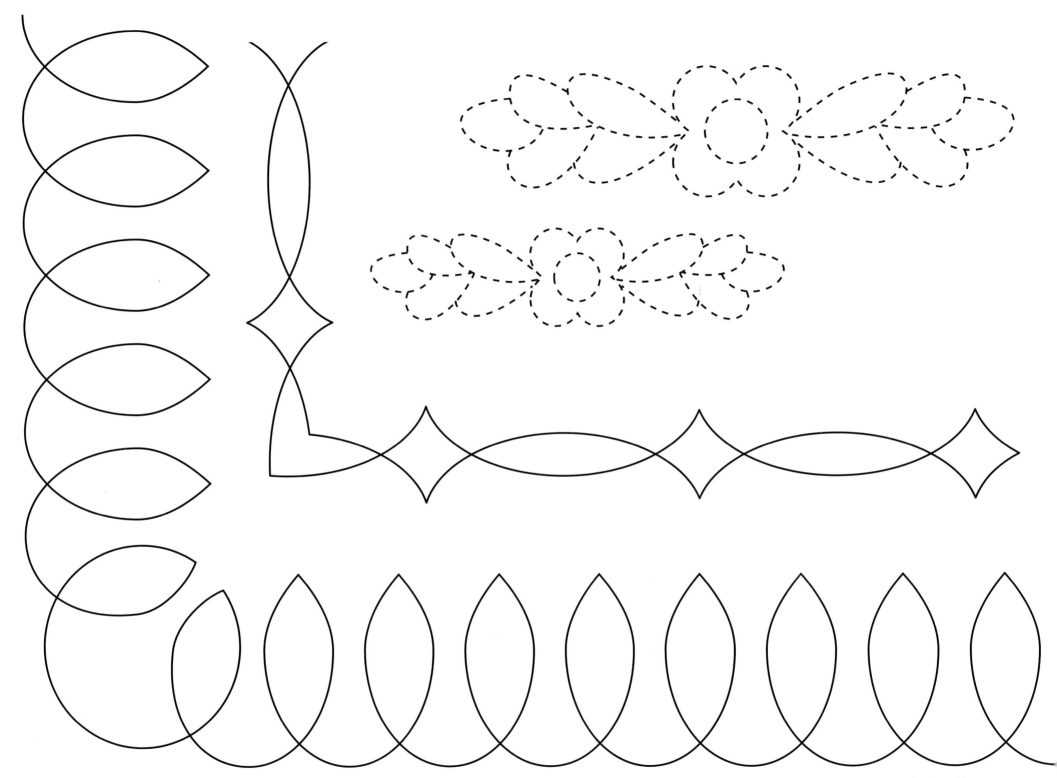

by **Cheryl Barnes** – *The Best of* **Shirley Thompson** Quilting Patterns

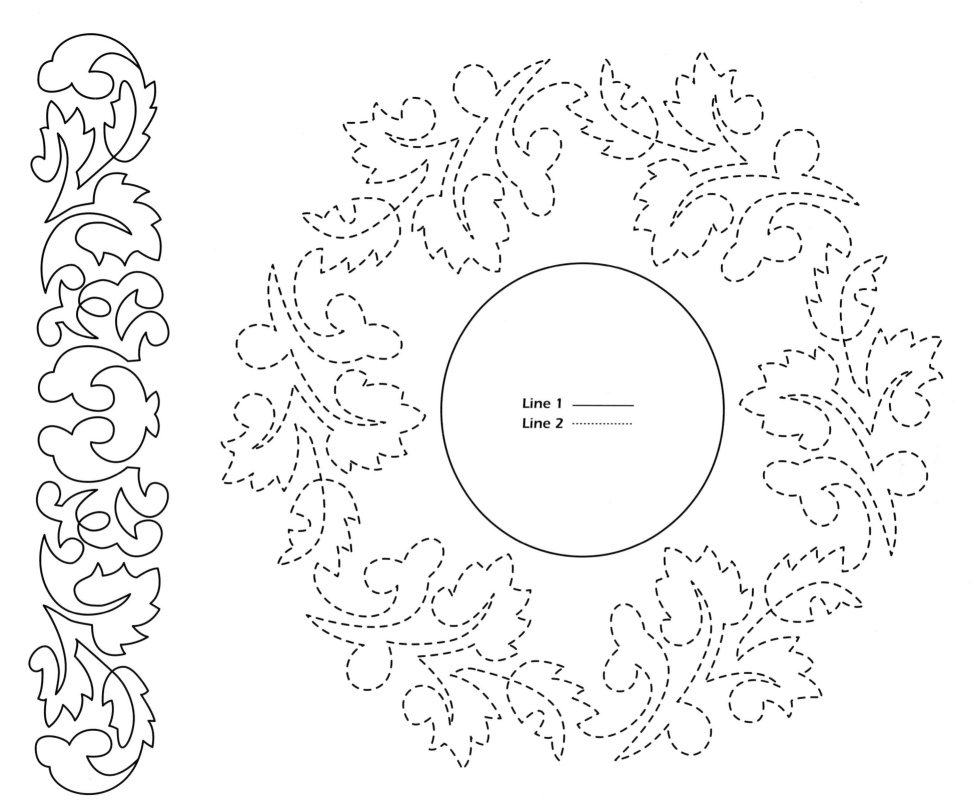

Line 1 ——————
Line 2 ································

Registration marks keep
the pattern straight.

Repeat for
border design
reversed at center

Adapted from an Egyptian textile motif

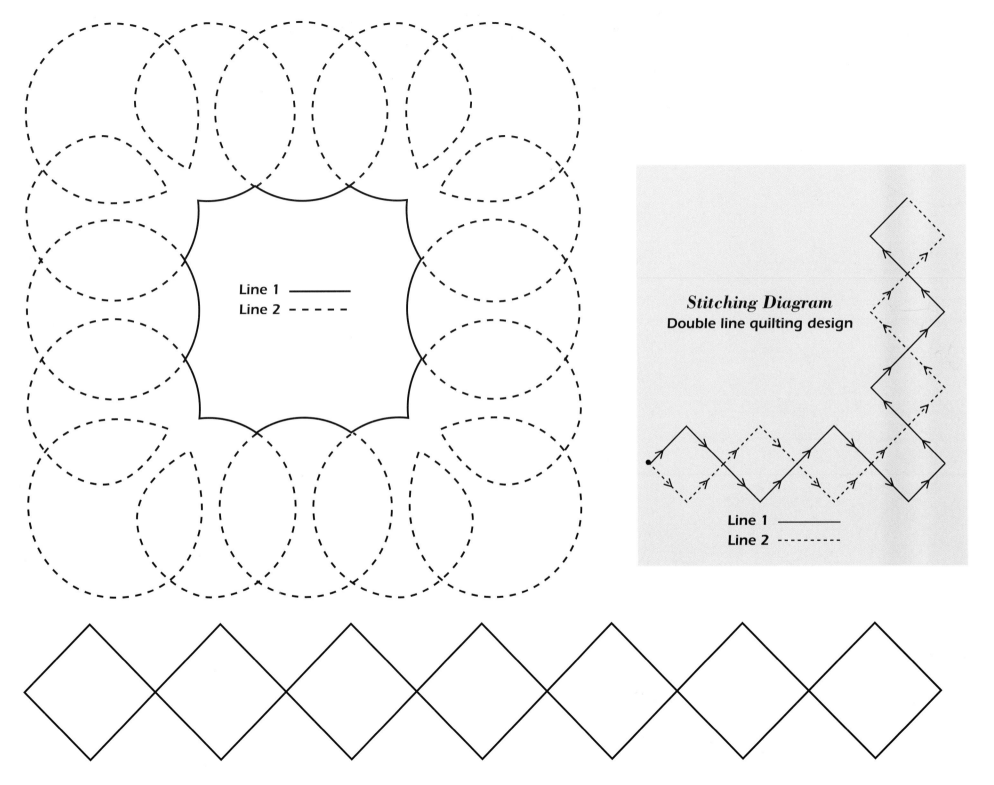

Line 1 ——————
Line 2 – – – – –

Stitching Diagram
Double line quilting design

Line 1 ——————
Line 2 – – – – –

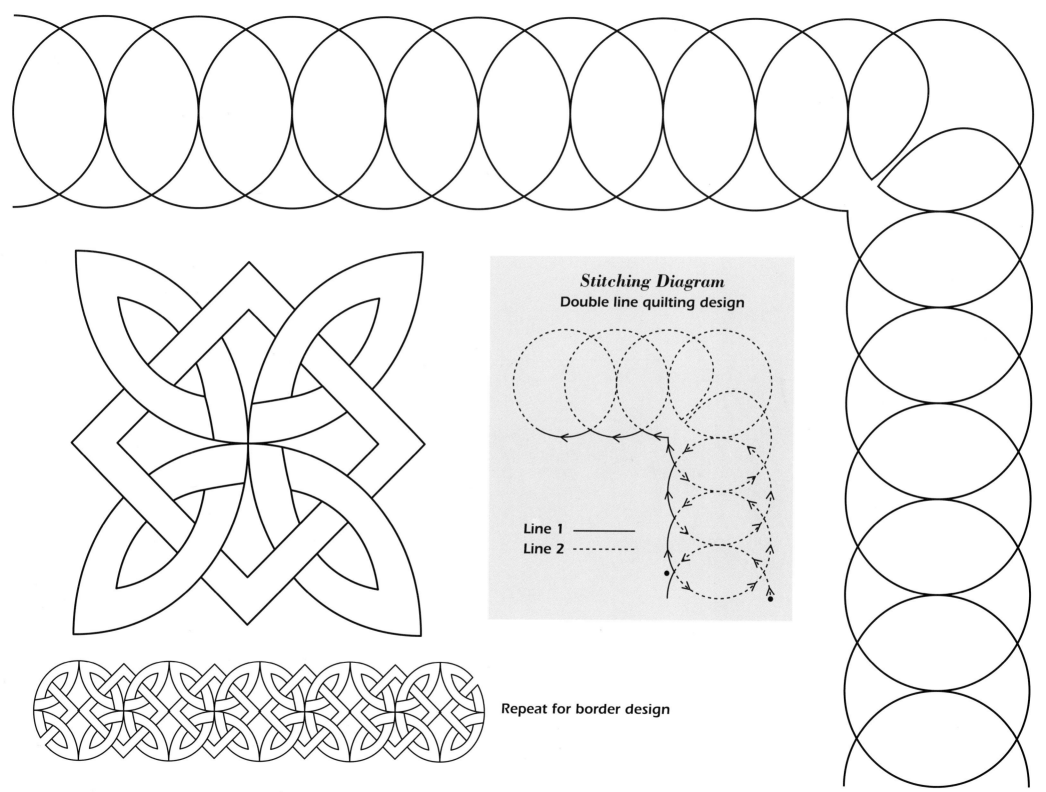

Stitching Diagram
Double line quilting design

Line 1 ——————
Line 2 - - - - - - -

Repeat for border design

reverse
at center

Line 1 ——————
Line 2 - - - - - -

by **Cheryl Barnes** – *The Best of* **Shirley Thompson** Quilting Patterns

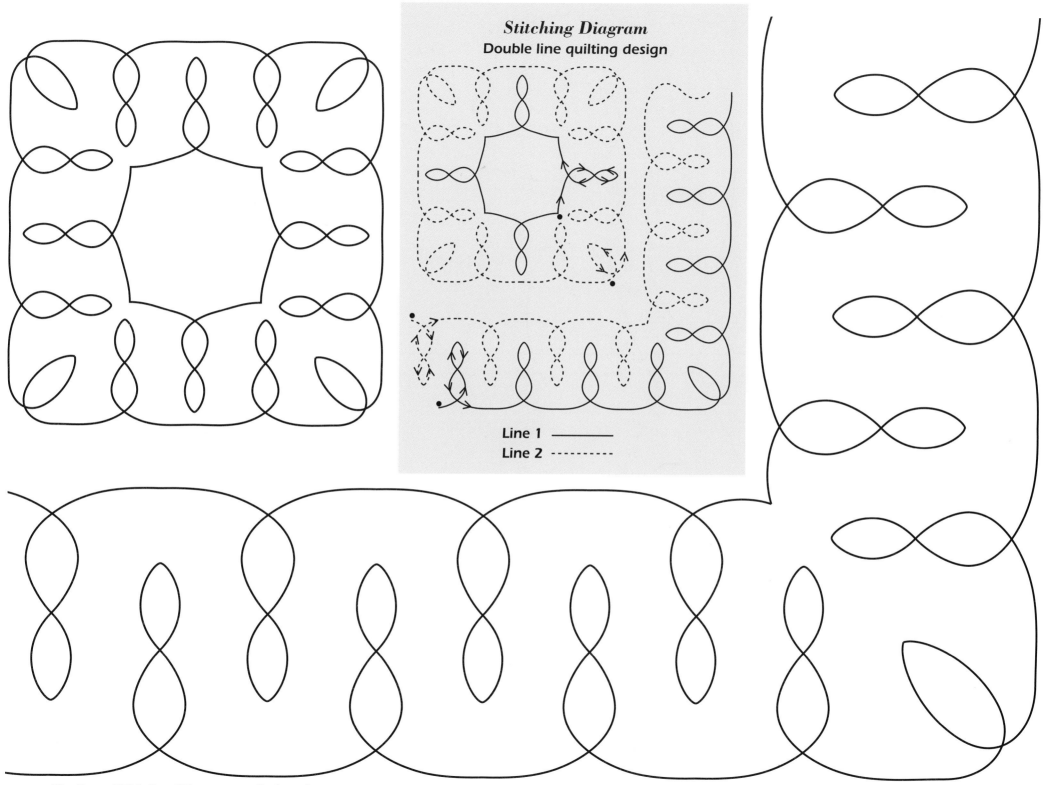

Stitching Diagram
Double line quilting design

Line 1 ———
Line 2 --------

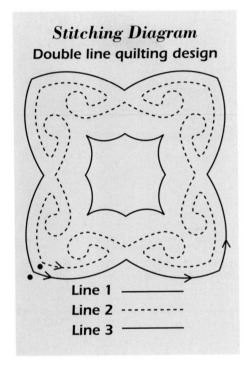

Stitching Diagram
Double line quilting design

Line 1 ——————
Line 2 - - - - - - - -
Line 3 ——————

Stitching Diagram
Double line quilting design

Line 1 ——————
Line 2 - - - - - -

by **Cheryl Barnes** – *The Best of* **Shirley Thompson** Quilting Patterns

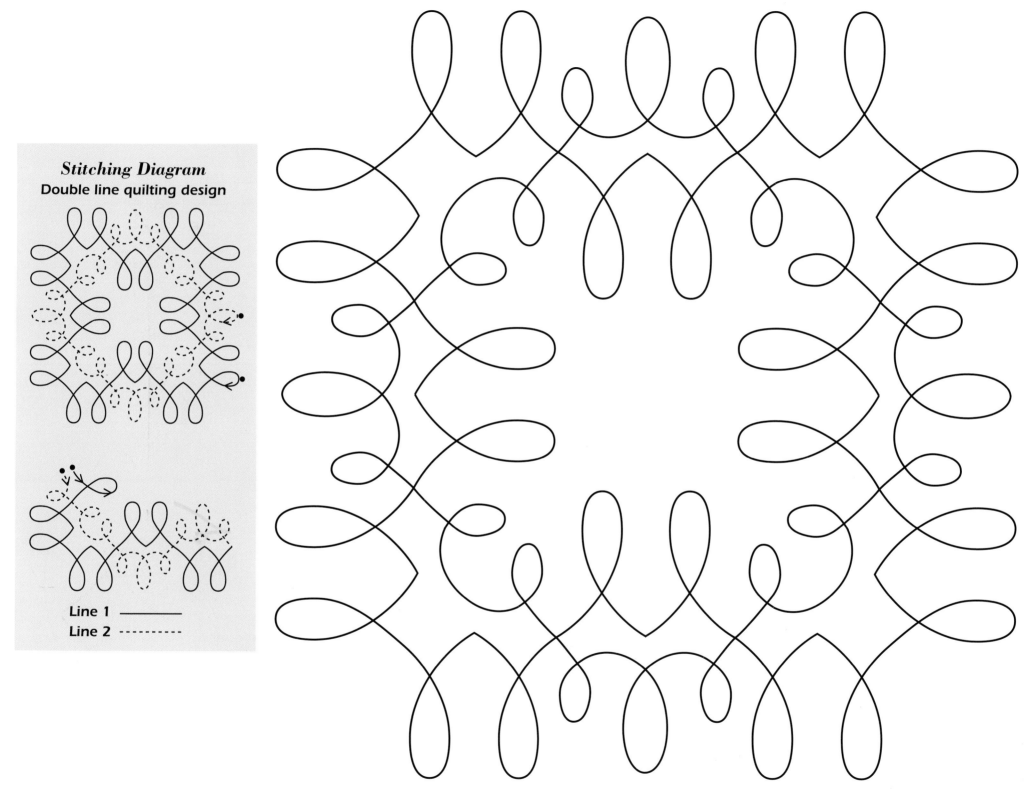

Stitching Diagram
Double line quilting design

Line 1 ————
Line 2 ------

2" border or lattice strip

by **Cheryl Barnes** – *The Best of* **Shirley Thompson** Quilting Patterns

by Cheryl Barnes – *The Best of* **Shirley Thompson** Quilting Patterns

The Best of **Shirley Thompson** Quilting Patterns – by **Cheryl Barnes**

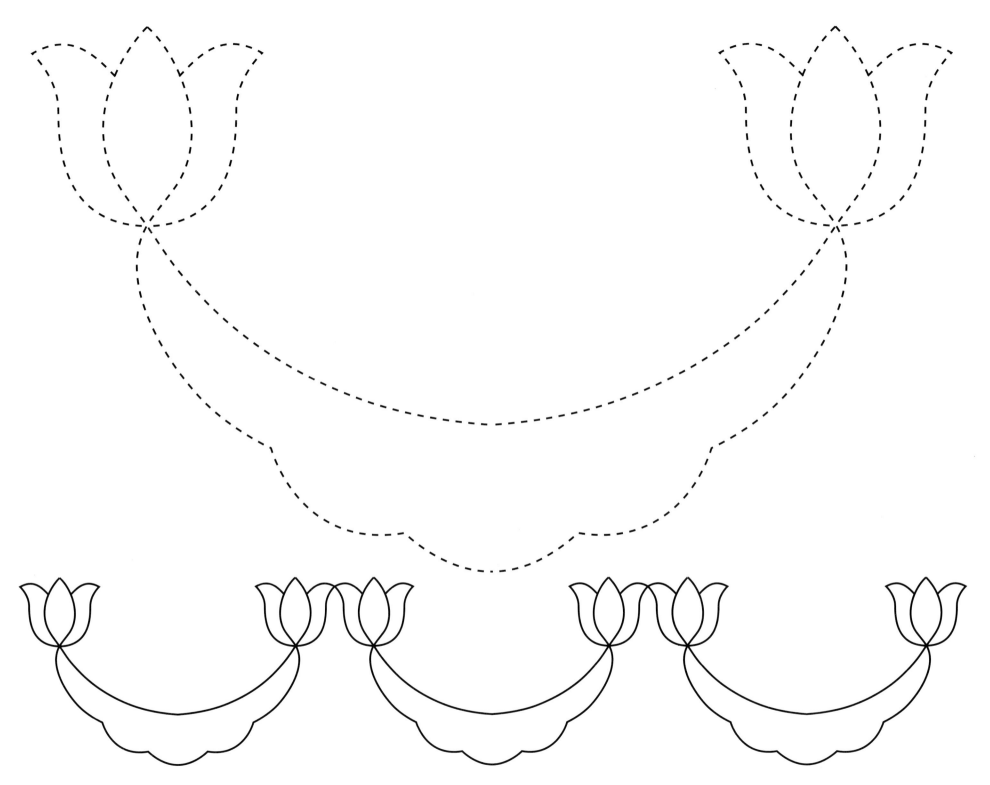

by **Cheryl Barnes** – *The Best of* **Shirley Thompson** Quilting Patterns

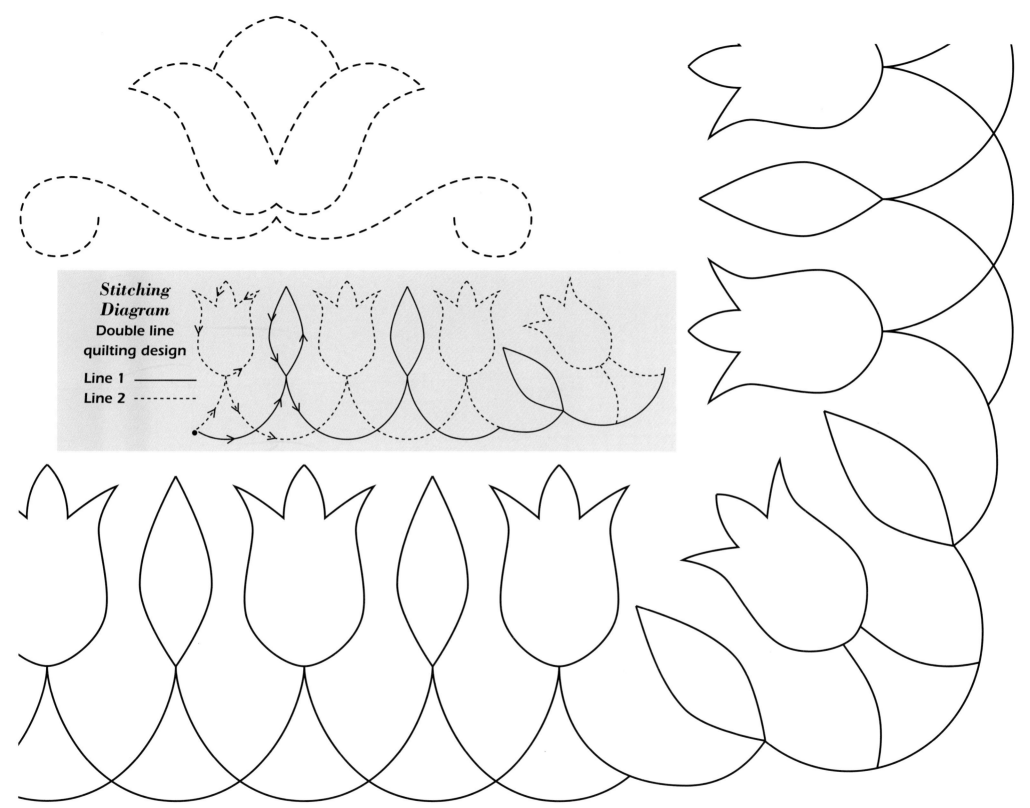

Stitching Diagram

Double line quilting design

Line 1 ———
Line 2 - - - -

Adapted from
the border design
shown below

by **Cheryl Barnes** – *The Best of* **Shirley Thompson** Quilting Patterns

44

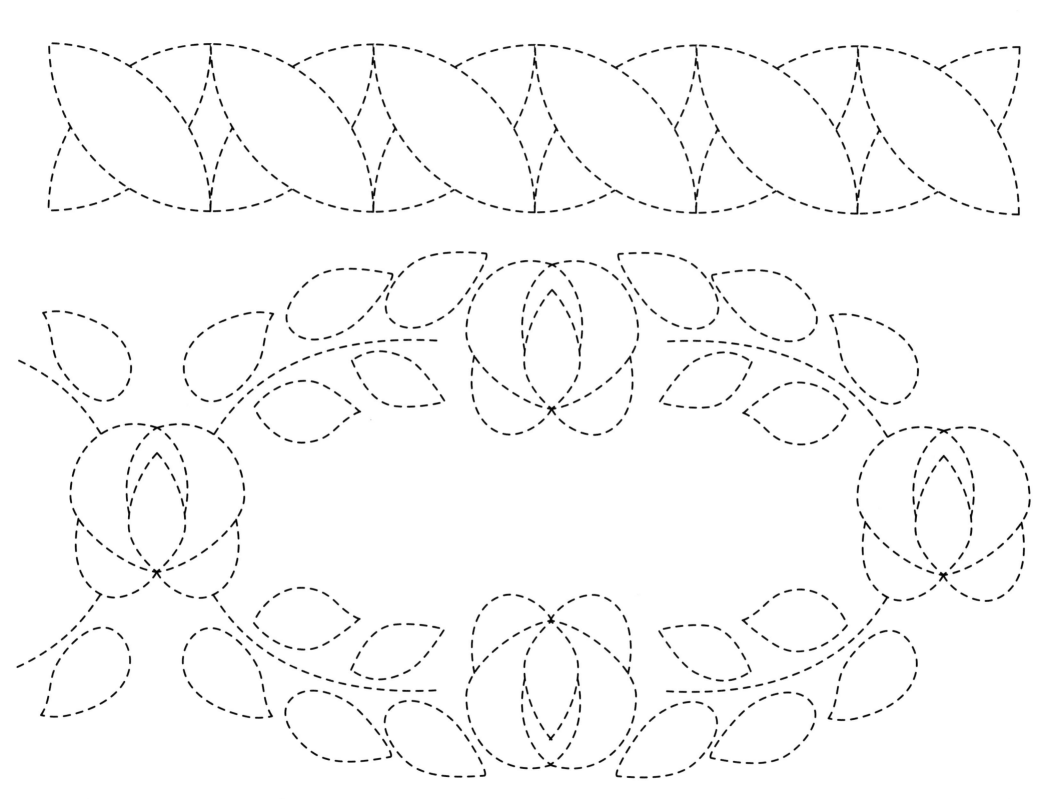

This design would be lovely quilted on the border of a bridal quilt.

Perfect for an appliqué motif

Quilting patterns
can be repeated
to make border
and block designs.

by **Cheryl Barnes** – *The Best of* **Shirley Thompson** Quilting Patterns

by **Cheryl Barnes** – *The Best of* **Shirley Thompson** Quilting Patterns

This quilting design is suitable for the Double Wedding Ring Pattern.

This quilting design is suitable for the Double Wedding Ring Pattern.

Connect reversed
end piece to
make a full repeat
of the design.

This design can be quilted in the space above a fan.

by **Cheryl Barnes** – *The Best of* **Shirley Thompson** Quilting Patterns

Block set-on-point

Stitching Diagram
Double line quilting design

Line 1 ————
Line 2 - - - - - -

Details can easily be added, omitted or combined in any quilting design when using the Quilter's Assistant Proportional Scale.

Full size pattern on page 88.

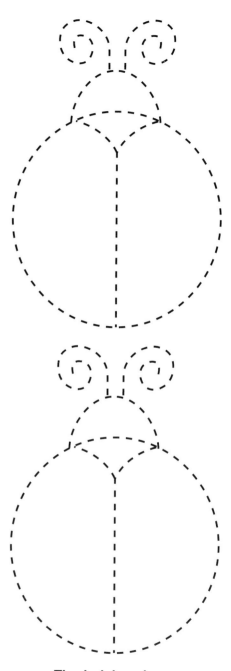

The ladybug is an appropriate quilting design for a border or lattice strips on a child's quilt.

Line 1 ——————
Line 2 - - - - - - -

Butterflies are perfect for quilts with a floral theme.

by **Cheryl Barnes** – *The Best of* **Shirley Thompson** Quilting Patterns

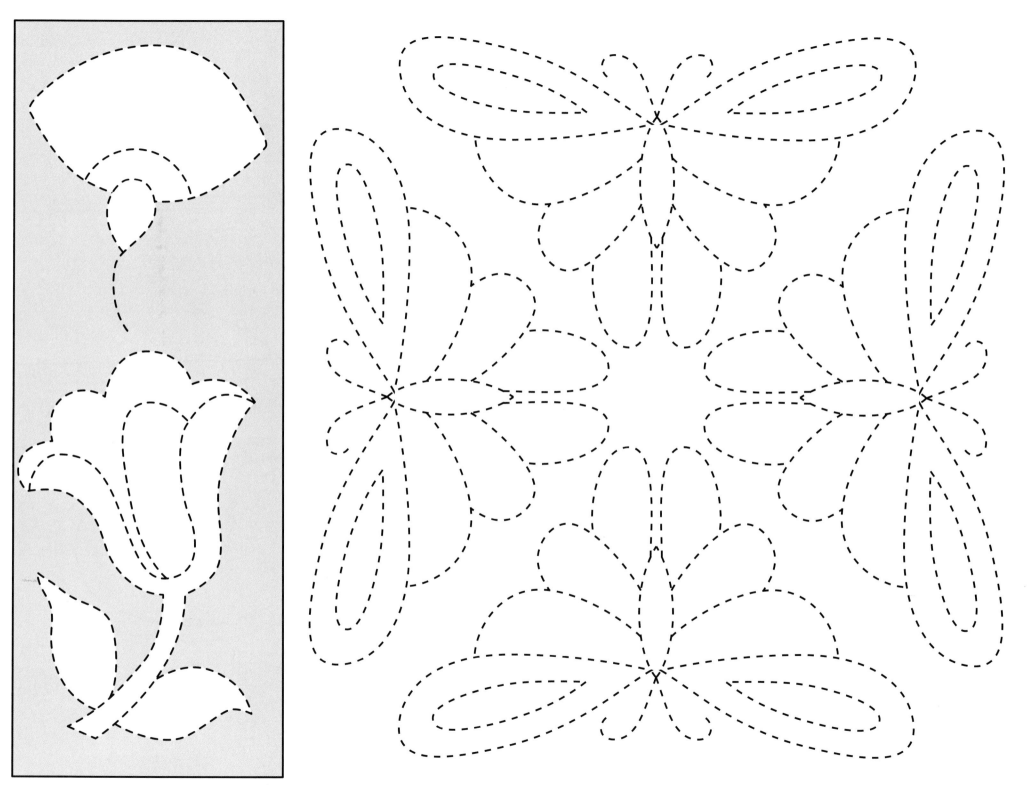

Line 1 ————
Line 2 --------

by Cheryl Barnes – *The Best of* **Shirley Thompson** Quilting Patterns

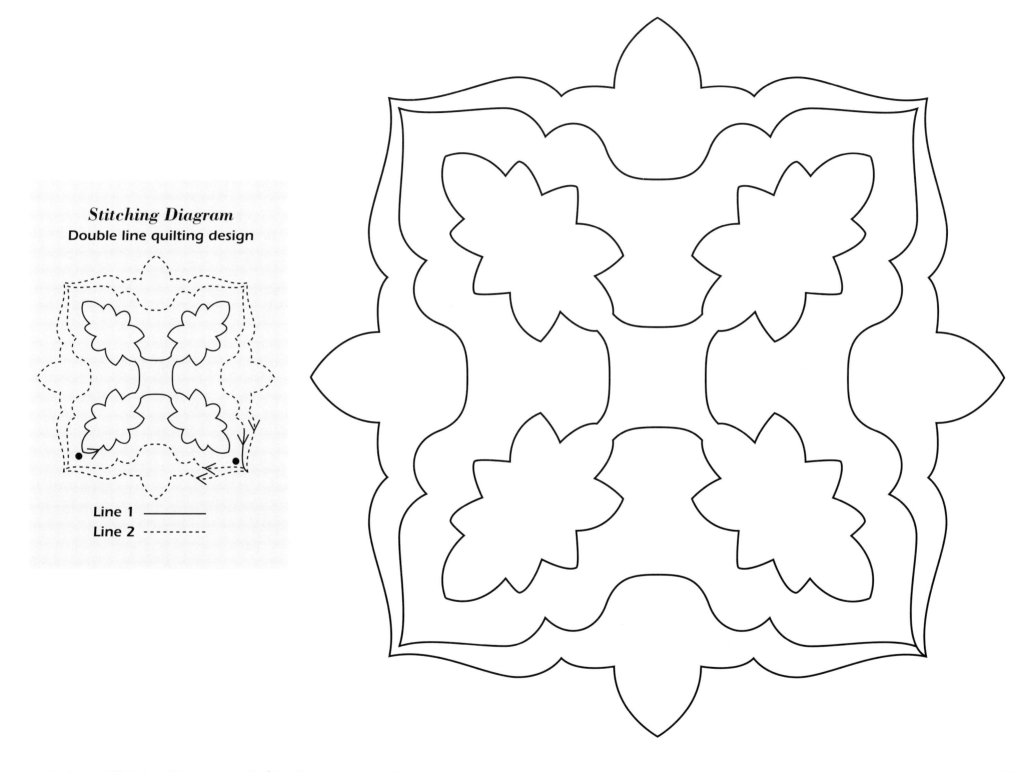

Stitching Diagram
Double line quilting design

Line 1 ——————
Line 2 - - - - - - -

Stitching Diagram
Single line quilting design

Stitching Diagram
Double line quilting design

Line 1 ——————
Line 2 - - - - - - -

Line 1 ——————
Line 2 - - - - - -

Stitching Diagram
Double line quilting design

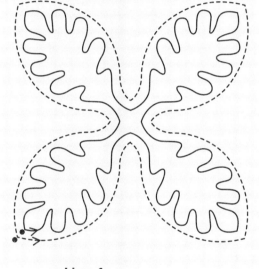

Line 1 ——————

Line 2 ------------

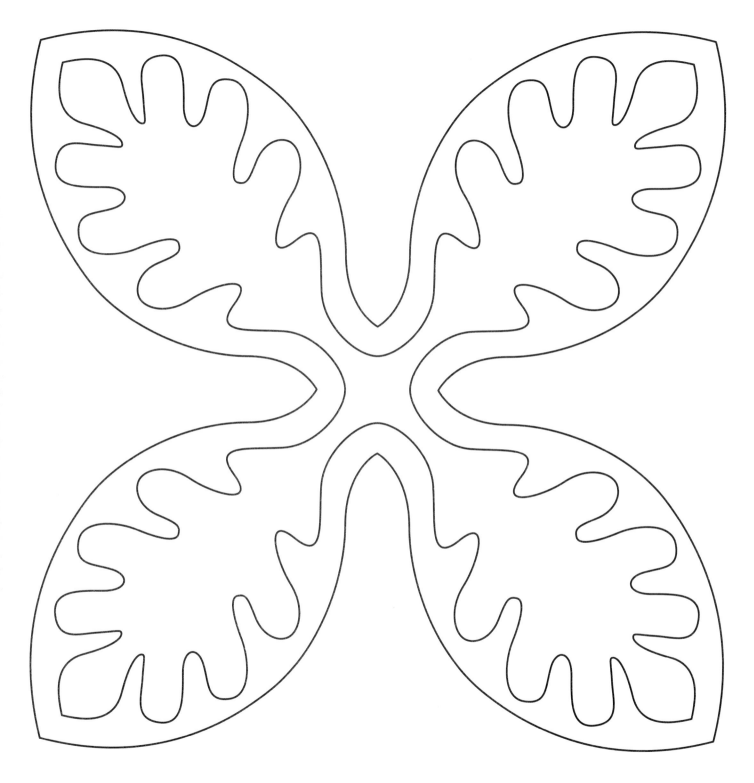

For continuous line quilting add dashed lines to the pattern.

For hand quilting add dashed lines to the pattern.

by **Cheryl Barnes** – *The Best of* **Shirley Thompson** Quilting Patterns

by **Cheryl Barnes** – *The Best of* **Shirley Thompson** Quilting Patterns

by **Cheryl Barnes** – *The Best of* **Shirley Thompson** Quilting Patterns

Multiple repeats
create new designs.

by Cheryl Barnes – *The Best of* **Shirley Thompson** Quilting Patterns

Stitching Diagram
Double line quilting design

Line 1 ———————
Line 2 - - - - - - -

Four repeats of the pattern
placed facing outward
make an outstanding design.

by **Cheryl Barnes** – *The Best of* **Shirley Thompson** Quilting Patterns

by **Cheryl Barnes** – *The Best of* **Shirley Thompson** Quilting Patterns

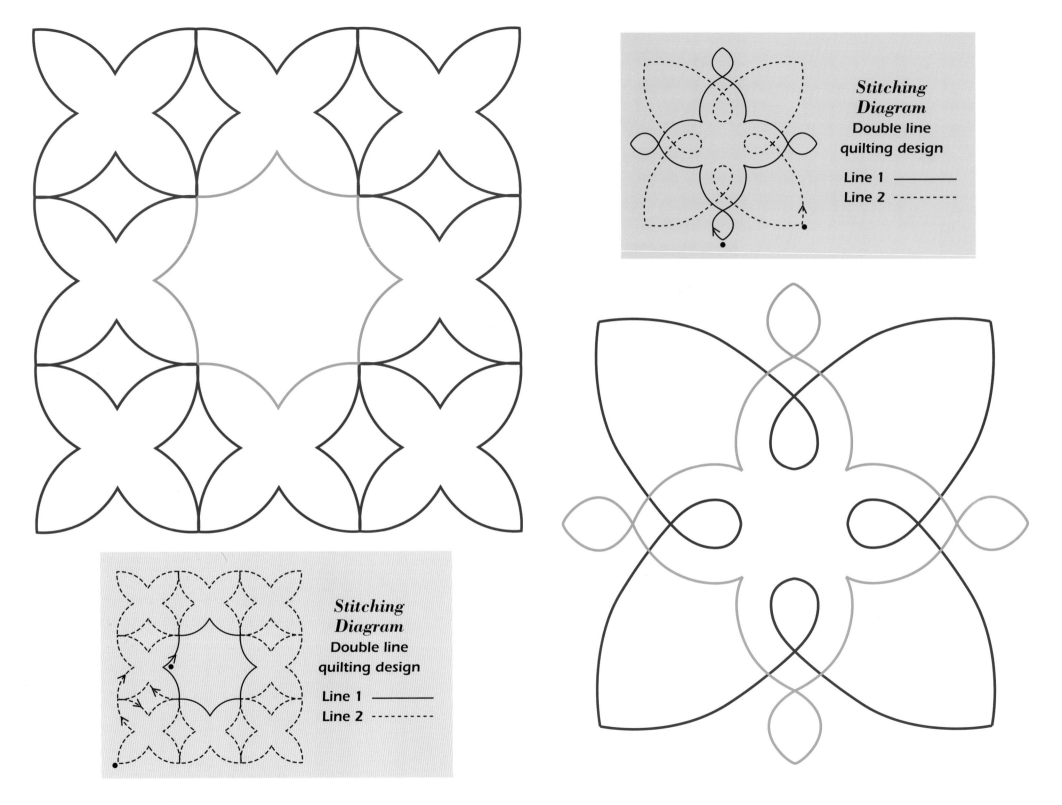

Stitching Diagram
Double line quilting design

Line 1 ——————
Line 2 - - - - - - -

Stitching Diagram
Double line quilting design

Line 1 ——————
Line 2 - - - - - - -

Finishing Touches for Perfect Quilting

Background or filler stitching done around a quilting pattern or applique' motif **creates a textured background and adds dimension.** Outline and echo stitches follow the shape of a previous line requiring no marking. Seed stitching/stippling/meandering fillers consist of wandering stitches and lines that do not cross or touch each other. Marking is required for accurate spacing and straight lines when using filler stitches such as fans, shells, diagonal cross hatching or hanging diamonds.

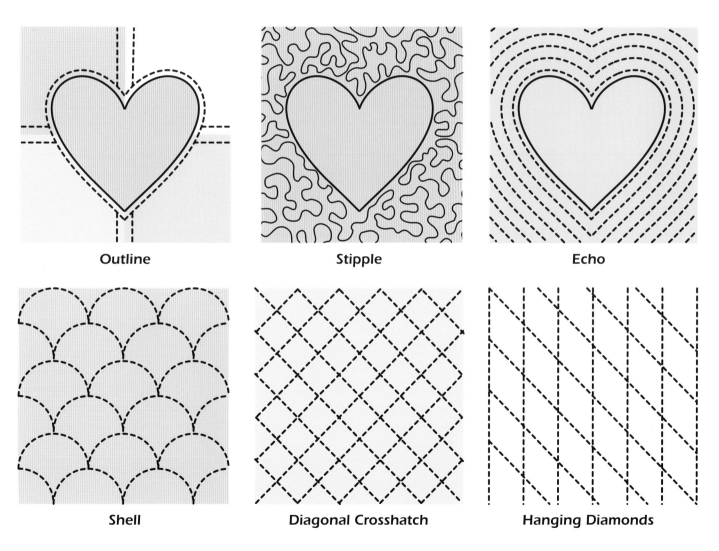

Outline

Stipple

Echo

Shell

Diagonal Crosshatch

Hanging Diamonds

Outline stitching is the most common form of quilting. To outline patchwork, follow the piece in the pattern and quilt about ¼ inch from the seam line. To outline appliqué, quilt very close to the shape itself.

Needle & Thread Tips

- Machine and hand quilters should always use new needles and change needles often. They are inexpensive but make a world of difference in the quality of stitching.

- Hand quilting needles, called betweens, are short strong needles that do not bend easily and come in a variety of sizes. Many quilters find that using a smaller-sized needle allows them to obtain smaller stitches.

- Hand quilting thread is pre-waxed 100 percent cotton thread that is available in a variety of colors. The wax strengthens the thread and keeps it from knotting. To eliminate tangling when stitching, knot the thread on the end that comes off the spool last.

- Machine-quilting needles also come in graduated sizes. The needle used is determined by the type and weight of the thread. Choose the smallest needle size that still allows the thread to pass through the needle eye without binding or sticking. Caution – if the needle is too small, the thread will fray as you stitch. Check your machine instruction book for recommendations.

- Machine-quilting thread is available in a vast selection of colors and fibers from cotton, rayon, polyester, silk, and blends. The thread selected should match the quality of the fabric and the type of batting used. Remember, the stitching needs to last as long as the life of the quilt, so do not use old thread that has been in your supplies forever!

- Beginning quilters should match the color of the quilting thread to the fabric, so uneven stitches are less visible. Stitching around curves often 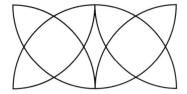 causes the tension to be less than perfect, pulling the bottom thread to the top or vice versa. Matching the color of the top and bobbin threads will make this imperfection less noticeable.

Thread has become an important design tool to be added to the arsenal of techniques that will enhance the finished quilt.

- Consider the following when **selecting threads:**

    1. *Will the quilting be done by hand or machine?*
    2. *Are you an experienced quilter?*
    3. *How will the quilt be used?*
    4. *Do you want the stitching to be prominent or blend with the fabric and create dimension?*
    5. *Should you use more than one color? Variegated colors? Or, metallic threads to add a bold new look?*

- Auditioning a variety of thread options is always time well spent. Thread wound on the spool will look different than when it is viewed on the fabric, Therefore, pull several yards of thread from the spool and place it in a loose pile on the quilt top. Move the thread pile and view all the fabrics used in the quilt top or stitch several lines of each option on a piece of fabric from the quilt. Choose the threads you like the best.

Backing Tips

- Backing fabric should be the same quality and weight as the fabric used to piece the top. Purchase yardage for the backing at the same time the other fabric is chosen to guarantee compatibility. Backing fabric is now available in widths up to 108 inches. Check your favorite quilt shop.

- Prints or multicolored fabrics are great choices to camouflage the quilting stitches of beginning quilters or if your project will have multiple changes of thread color.

- Solid fabrics or tone-on-tone fabrics are good choices if you are using a thread that blends with the fabric. This often creates a quilt back as lovely as a wholecloth quilt.

- Prewash the backing fabric if the quilt top fabric has been prewashed. Measure and piece after washing. The backing should be at least four inches larger on all sides than the top.

- If the backing is to be pieced from full yardage, place the full width of the fabric in the center and add an equal amount of fabric panels to each side to reach the required size. Avoid placing a seam along the center back where the quilt is most often folded, as this will prevent excess wear.

- "Back Art" is created when the quilting is planned, taking into consideration placement on both the front and the back. The back can be pieced creating a reversible quilt, or it can be solid, creating a wholecloth effect. Back art requires precise planning and can be time consuming and challenging, as well as rewarding. Make sure the end use of the quilt will justify the time and effort it takes to accomplish.

Batting Tips

- Batting is the filler sandwiched between the quilt top and backing which provides warmth, gives the quilt body, and adds dimension. Always buy the best quality batting that is available.

- There is a large selection of battings that can be purchased in packages or by the yard. Options include black, white, bleached, unbleached, needle punched, with or without scrim. Thicknesses (loft) range from very thin (⅛") to very thick (2"). Fibers include cotton, polyester, wool, silk, flannel, and poly/cotton blends. Fusible batting is a timesaver, and perfect for beginners or when working with large quilts. (See Resources, page 110.)

Read the information on the package to choose the proper batt. The package will supply recommendations for hand/machine quilting, washing directions, and the amount/spacing of the stitches required to eliminate bunching and shifting.

- Consider the following when *choosing batting:*

  1. *Will the quilt be hand or machine quilted?*
  2. *Is warmth a factor or is this a summer quilt?*
  3. *How will the quilt be used? Will it be washed frequently?*
  4. *Is there a preference for natural or synthetic fibers?*
  5. *Are quilting patterns chosen within the suggested spacing?*

- The machine quilting process causes shrinkage in the length and width of the batting. Measure the quilt top and add 4 inches on each side, more if a heavy amount of quilting will be done. If the type of batting indicates pre-washing, measure and cut after washing.

- To relax a folded batt, take the batting out of the bag and lay it flat for a day before layering the quilt. To quickly remove wrinkles, tumble batting (out of the bag) in a cool dryer for a few minutes. A hair dryer set on warm (not hot) held over the flat batting will also help it to relax.

Basting Tips

The quilt sandwich consists of the quilt top, batting, and backing and must be layered and basted before you can begin quilting. This step is essential to insure that the quilt remains secure during the quilting process and avoids puckers and folds.

1. Work on a large table, floor, or other flat surface that accommodates the size of the project. Practice the first time on a small project.

2. Press the top and backing to remove wrinkles and clip all loose threads. Fold the top, back, and batting separately into quarters, and mark the center points with safety pins.

3. Begin by spreading the backing fabric wrong side up, keeping it flat without stretching. Secure to a flat surface by clipping to the edge of a table with binder clips, taping the backing to the floor, or pinning the backing fabric to carpet.

4. Place the batting on top of the backing, matching center pins and smoothing flat. Adjust binding clips, tape, or pins to secure the batting. Remove both pins marking the center of the batting and the backing..

5. Place the quilt top right side up on top of the batting. Check to see that it is centered and straight along the top, while allowing the margin of extra batting and backing on all four sides. Remove the center pin and secure with clips or tape before basting.

- **Thread basting** is done with a large darning needle and a simple running stitch about 2 inches long. Start by basting diagonal lines radiating out from the center, finish by basting around the outer edge. If working on a large project, consider securing the layers first with large straight pins to hold layers secure as they are handled.

- **Pin basting** is accomplished with curved pins of different sizes that resemble safety pins. Begin inserting the pins at one end of the quilt, spacing them 3-6 inches apart, row by row. Do not close the pins until all are inserted. Use the edge of a serrated grapefruit spoon to speed this process and avoid sore fingers.

- **Tacking tools** have a gun-like appearance with a very sharp needle. It uses plastic tacks with a ¼" – ½" inch shank to hold the layers of the quilt together.

- **Quilting machines** (Shortarm, longarm) Baste quilts on quilting systems using the loading technique called "Floating the Top." Pin the backing and batting to the take up leader. Place the quilt top over the batting leaving at least 4 inches of margin on each side. The grip of the batting is usually enough to hold the quilt top in place while basting.

- **Spray Basting** is quick and easy with a temporary spray adhesive such as 404 Spray and Fix. Spray between each layer as you create the quilt sandwich. (See Resources, page 110.)

Quilt Labels

- Quilt labels provide a record of the quilter's handiwork. It guarantees that the information about the quilt is passed on to generations of family members and quilters far into the future. If the quilt has not been signed on the front, add a label on the back of the quilt.

- The label should contain the following information: name(s) of the quiltmaker, when and where it was made, as well as the name of the quilt. If it is a gift, include the name(s) of the recipient and for what occasion the quilt was made. Use complete names, dates, and places.

Consider the following before *making a quilt label:*

1. *A quilt label can be a block made from muslin, a preprinted label, or a block pieced from the quilt top fabric.*

2. *Lettering can be hand embroidered or marked with a permanent fabric pen. For accurate lettering and spacing it helps to print your information on the computer in your chosen font. Then use a light box to trace onto your label.*

3. *Appliqué the label onto the back of the quilt if the quilt has already been quilted. Stitching the label to the backing fabric before you start quilting will insure that the label becomes a permanent part of the quilt.*

- Make a bag from coordinating fabric, for gift giving or storing the quilt. This can be a simple pillowcase pattern tied with a pretty ribbon. Save the scraps from the quilt to keep in the bag to aid with any unforeseen repair in the future.

Appliqué patterns for quilt labels can be made from any quilting design.

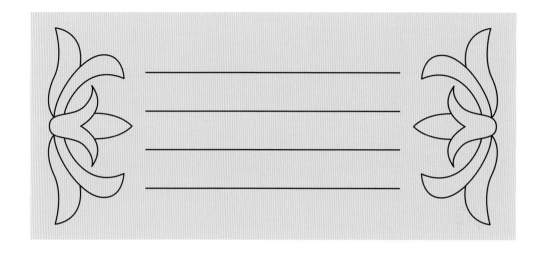

Free–Motion Quilting Tips

- Free-motion quilting allows the quilter the freedom to stitch in any direction, while following the stitching path of beautiful flowing quilting patterns. Think of free-motion quilting as drawing with needle and thread. The machine will need a few adjustments to allow free-motion quilting.

- Consider the following when *making adjustments:*

   1. *Install a darning or quilting foot to the machine.*
   2. *Drop/disengage the feed dogs or cover with template plastic or a business card. Tape in place and cut a small hole to match the needle hole opening.*
   3. *Use the needle down option, so the needle will remain in the fabric when the quilter stops stitching.*

- Some quilters feel out of control stitching with the feed dogs down. Another option is keeping the feed dogs up, but releasing the pressure on the quilting foot. Gradually adjust the pressure until the setting allows freedom of movement with the needed control.

- The stitch length is determined by the combination of the speed of stitching and the movement of the fabric. Every quilter has their own quilting speed – experiment with different speeds and movements until you find what feels most natural.

- Watch for stitches that are too long or curved lines that look square. To fix this, increase the machine speed and slow down the movement of the fabric/hands. If the stitches are too small and the thread frequently breaks, decrease the machine speed and increase the movement of the fabric/hands.

- Beginning machine quilters or those who do not quilt regularly should schedule practice sessions of about 15–20 minutes a day for a week before starting on a project. Put together several small practice blocks using the same fabric and batting as the quilt. Compare the results at the end of the week to the first practice stitches.

- Warm up before each quilting session on the actual quilt, to insure a consistent quality of stitching. While quilting, take breaks to relax and stretch your neck, arms, and shoulders.

- Roll or accordion fold the quilt and secure with clamps, exposing only the area being stitched. Decrease the drag caused by the weight of a large quilt by draping the unquilted length over the shoulder and positioning the sewing table up against a wall supporting the quilted length.

- Following the stitching path is easier after tracing it several times before quilting it. Sally Terry teaches this technique as *The Five Shapes of Quilting,* in her book *Pathways to Better Quilting* (AQS, 2004). You will find these shapes in almost every quilting pattern. Combined they form thousands of patterns.

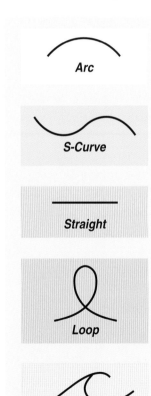

Arc

S-Curve

Straight

Loop

Hook

Sally Terry's Five Shapes of Quilting

In an excerpt from her book *Pathways to Better Quilting,* Sally states

"It is amazing to me that no matter whether you use a longarm, midarm, shortarm, or traditional sewing machine, my stitching concepts apply to all methods of quilting. The following pathways will enable all of you to quickly and easily stitch any design on the quilt sandwich."

By practicing the five shapes, you will develop "cell memory" and learn that you have the freedom to create and execute any quilting pattern.

Hand Quilting Tips

- Hand quilting requires only a few tools, the right thimble, needles, thread and hoop/frame. Many hours are spent hand quilting so finding the right combination is essential to enjoying the unhurried, relaxing process of hand quilting.

- Quilting hoops and frames make hand quilting easier and keep the fabric from pleating or puckering. Traditional quilting hoops come in a variety of sizes and the hoop is held in one hand while stitching. The lap hoop has a base that sits on the quilter's lap, freeing both hands for stitching. The added advantage to both is the ability to rotate your project allowing you to always quilt towards yourself.

- The thimble is worn on the middle finger of the sewing hand and is available in metal, plastic, or leather, as well as paddle thimbles that are held, not worn. It is helpful to ask other hand quilters what they like about their favorite thimble.

- Consider the following options *before quilting:*

  1. *Take a class, watch a demo, or get a book that teaches the various methods of completing the hand quilting stitch.*

  2. *The traditional rocking stitch stacks several stitches on the needle before pulling through the fabric.*

  3. *Stab stitching is inserting the needle directly down through the fabric, moving forward your chosen stitch length, and reinserting the needle through to the top.*

  4. *Thumb quilting requires a thumb thimble with dimples on the sides. It is the stitch most often used by quilters stitching on a floor frame, because it enables you to stitch in all directions without turning your work.*

- New hand quilters should concentrate on mastering one skill at a time. First practice stitching in a straight line. Next, concentrate on making the stitches even, and lastly focus on the size of the stitch. It is more important that the stitches be straight and even than painfully small.

- Refer to Needle & Thread Tips on page 104. Thread the needle by holding it so only the tip is exposed and then setting the eye of the needle on the thread. This is called "needling the thread" versus threading the needle. Thread 8-10 needles at a time, storing them in a pincushion to save stitching time.

- Hide knots by inserting the needle into the quilt about an inch from where quilting will begin. Go through the top and the batting only, bringing the needle up at the point where the quilting will begin. Gently tug on the thread to pop the knot through the top, securing it in the batting. End your thread when done stitching in the same manner.

- Warming up on a practice piece before working on the actual project will insure that your stitches are more consistent in length. This is especially important if it has been a long period of time since your last quilting session.

Resources

Products:

The Best of Shirley Thompson
    Continuous Block & Border Sets Companion Pack
Golden Threads Quilting Paper
Quilter's Assistant Proportional Scale
Pathways to Better Quilting Book
Pathways to Better Quilting Companion Pack
Golden Threads
2 S. 373 Seneca Drive, Wheaton, IL 60187
888-477-7718
www.goldenthreads.com ▪ info@goldenthreads.com

Books by Shirley Thompson:

Think Small
Tried & True
Old-Time Quilting Designs
Designs for Continuous Line Quilting
Quilts Start to Finish
Powell Publications
2 S. 373 Seneca Drive, Wheaton, IL 60187
888-477-7718
www.goldenthreads.com ▪ info@goldenthreads.com

Fusible Batting:

Heirlooom Fusible Cotton Blend Batting
Hobbs Bonded Fibers
PO Box 2521, Waco, TX 76702
254-741-0040

Temporary Adhesive Spray:

404 Spray and Fix
J.T. Trading Company
3 Simms Lane, Newtown, CT 06470
230-270-7744

Bibliography

Halgrimson, Jan and Thompson, Shirley. *Quilts Start to Finish.*
Powell Publications,1997.

Terry, Sally. *Pathways to Better Quilting.*
American Quilter's Society and Golden Threads, 2003.

Thompson, Shirley. *Designs for Continuous Line Quilting.*
Powell Publications, 1993.

Thompson, Shirley. *The Finishing Touch.*
Powell Publications,1980.

Thompson, Shirley. *It's Not a Quilt Until It's Quilted.*
Powell Publications, 1984.

Thompson, Shirley. *Old-Time Quilting Designs.*
Powell Publications, 1988.

Thompson, Shirley. *Think Small.*
Powell Publications, 1988.

Thompson, Shirley. *Tried and True.*
Powell Publications, 1987.

**Visit your local quilt shop for the latest in:
needles, threads, backing, batting,
thimbles, hoops, frames and labels.**

About the Author

With a love of hand needlework of all types from early childhood, Cheryl Barnes discovered machine quilting and purchased a longarm machine in 1994. She began her own quilting business, Golden Threads, at that time.

After quilting for several years, Cheryl felt limited by the lack of new patterns available to longarm quilters. The pursuit of building a library of quilting designs took Cheryl's company from quilting to publishing quilting designs. She became acquainted with the quilting designs by Keryn Emmerson of Australia, who was searching for a publisher that would service the longarm industry. Golden Threads continues to publish originally designed quilting patterns from prominent United States and Australian artists.

Cheryl and her husband, Jim, also own Powell Publications. They purchased the company in 2002, which expanded their listing of designers and patterns. The broad range of products all focused on quilting patterns makes their business unique. Stencils, pantographs, pattern packs, books, quilted garments, and notions enable them to service all quilters – from hand or sewing machine quilters to those with home quilting systems or longarm machines. With a broad range of talented designers, each with their own style, they are sure to have something that appeals to every quilter.

Residing in Illinois, Cheryl and Jim work full time in the business. Their three sons have all participated in the family business, rolling pantographs, filling orders, taking inventory, and occasionally attending quilt shows. The company continues to expand through a new pattern and technique book series published in cooperation with the American Quilter's Society.

Other ◆AQS◆ Books

This is only a small selection of the books available from the American Quilter's Society. AQS books are known worldwide for timely topics, clear writing, beautiful color photos, and for accurate illustrations and patterns. The following books are available from your local bookseller or quilt shop.

#6419   US$24.95

#6069   US$24.95

#6294 US$21.95

#6299   US$24.95

#6006   US$25.95

#6509   US$22.95

LOOK for these books nationally.

CALL 1-800-626-5420 or VISIT our

Web Site at www.americanquilter.com

⅋G Products